Freeman's Legendary Walk-Off: A World Series Moment to Remember

How Freddie Freeman's Grand Slam Transformed World Series History and Electrified Dodger Stadium

Elena Ellsworth

Table of Contents

Chapter 3: The Build-Up to the Grand Slam

Late-Game Drama: Defensive Brilliance and Costly Mistakes

Strategic Calls: Bringing in Nestor Cortes

Freddie Freeman's Resolve: Playing Through Pain

Chapter 4: The Walk-Off Grand Slam

Analyzing the At-Bat: Freeman vs. Cortes

The Swing That Shocked the World: Crowd and Stadium Reaction

Making History: The First Walk-Off Slam in World Series History

Chapter 5: The Aftermath and Reactions

Post-Game Insights: Freeman, Teammates, and Dave Roberts Speak Out

Yankees' Reflection: Aaron Boone's Decisions Under Scrutiny

The Moment That Broke the Internet: Media and Fan Reactions

Introduction

Setting the Stage: Dodgers vs. Yankees in the 2024 World Series

The 2024 World Series brought baseball fans a dream matchup: the Los Angeles Dodgers and the New York Yankees. These two storied franchises, steeped in history and success, reignited a rivalry that has captivated generations. Each team arrived at this stage with something to prove— the Dodgers looking to solidify their recent dominance in the National League, and the Yankees eager to reassert their place as baseball royalty after years of rebuilding.

Dodger Stadium, bathed in a sea of blue under a crisp autumn sky, provided the perfect backdrop for the opener of what promised to be an unforgettable series. Fans poured into the stadium, buzzing with anticipation. The air was electric, charged with the weight of history and the promise of another chapter in the Dodgers-Yankees rivalry. This wasn't just another World Series game; it was a clash of titans, a battle between two teams with legacies that had shaped the very essence of Major League Baseball.

The Yankees, led by manager Aaron Boone, boasted a lineup blending youthful energy and seasoned veterans. Gerrit Cole, their ace, stood tall as the embodiment of their hopes. On the other side, Dave Roberts' Dodgers entered with an impressive roster and a relentless drive to capture the championship. Players like Freddie Freeman, Mookie Betts, and Clayton Kershaw symbolized the team's enduring quest for greatness.

The Legacy of Game 1 Moments in Baseball History

Game 1 of a World Series often sets the tone, and history has shown how pivotal it can be. Iconic moments from past Game 1 encounters linger in the minds of fans and players alike. Who could forget Kirk Gibson's dramatic walk-off home run in the 1988 World Series, a moment that cemented his legacy as a Dodgers legend? Similarly, the Yankees have had their share of heroics, from Reggie Jackson's clutch performances in the late 1970s to Derek Jeter's leadership during the dynasty years.

These moments are more than just highlights—they are symbols of resilience, grit, and the raw drama that baseball delivers. They inspire new generations of players to rise to the occasion, to chase glory and etch their names into the annals of the sport.

The stage was set for another such moment in 2024. Both teams knew the stakes, and the players understood the gravity of the opportunity before them. For fans, this was a chance to witness history, to see their heroes rise or fall. The Dodgers and

Yankees weren't just competing for a trophy; they were vying for immortality in the game's storied history.

Chapter 1: The Road to the Fall Classic

The Dodgers' and Yankees' Journey Through the Regular Season

The 2024 regular season was a tale of dominance, resilience, and strategic brilliance for both the Los Angeles Dodgers and the New York Yankees. These two powerhouse teams each carved out their path to the World Series, overcoming challenges that tested their depth and determination.

For the Dodgers, the season was one of consistency and firepower. With a lineup that boasted some of the most dynamic players in baseball, including Mookie Betts, Freddie Freeman, and Clayton Kershaw, the team's performance was a display of both individual brilliance and collective strength. Their pitching staff, headlined by Kershaw and newcomer Julio Urías, provided stability and kept the team in contention throughout the season. The Dodgers' offense, known for its ability to explode at any moment, was relentless, producing runs in bunches. Despite some injury setbacks and the always-looming pressure of being a favorite, they managed to finish at the top of the National League, securing a crucial postseason berth.

The Yankees, on the other hand, experienced a more turbulent journey through the regular season. After a slow start, they began to hit their stride midway through, with the team's leadership and star power guiding them back to the top of the American League East. Aaron Judge's bat remained one of the most feared in the league, and Gerrit Cole's dominance on the mound proved pivotal in keeping the Yankees competitive. Their pitching rotation, bolstered by a strong bullpen, began to gel as the season progressed, and their lineup, filled with both young talent and seasoned veterans, became a force to be reckoned with. Although

injuries and inconsistency plagued them
throughout the year, the Yankees found their
rhythm and clinched the AL East title, setting the
stage for a dramatic playoff run.

Key Moments and Turning Points in the 2024 Playoffs

As both teams entered the postseason, they carried
with them the weight of a long and grueling regular
season. The playoffs were a true test of grit and
perseverance, with each team facing formidable
competition.

For the Dodgers, the National League Division
Series (NLDS) was a test of endurance. They faced a
tough challenge in the form of the Atlanta Braves, a
team that had been a powerhouse throughout the
regular season. It was here that the Dodgers proved
their mettle. They capitalized on key

moments—whether it was Betts stealing bases, Freeman's clutch hits, or the dominant pitching performances from Kershaw and the bullpen. Their ability to perform under pressure was the difference maker, and they advanced to the National League Championship Series (NLCS).

Meanwhile, the Yankees' road to the Fall Classic was marked by grit and the refusal to back down. They found themselves in a heated battle with the Houston Astros in the American League Division Series (ALDS). The series was a back-and-forth contest, with both teams showcasing their strengths. But the Yankees' timely hitting, especially from Judge, and Cole's consistency on the mound, propelled them past the Astros. In the ALCS, they faced a formidable opponent in the Toronto Blue Jays. With the series tied at 2-2, it was a critical Game 5 where the Yankees' veterans rose to the occasion, clinching the pennant in a thrilling win that sent them to the World Series.

Both teams' playoff journeys were full of highs and lows, but what they proved most was their resilience. They were battle-tested and ready for the ultimate stage: the World Series.

Freddie Freeman: Battling Injuries and Leading His Team

One of the most remarkable stories of the 2024 season was Freddie Freeman's leadership and perseverance in the face of adversity. Known for his consistent bat and leadership in the clubhouse, Freeman found himself battling through injuries that threatened to derail his season.

A lingering ankle issue had Freeman on the sidelines for a portion of the regular season, and at times, his mobility was compromised. But even when the injuries began to take a toll on his physical game, Freeman's mental toughness remained unshaken. He continued to contribute, playing through the pain and providing a steady presence in the lineup.

His leadership was invaluable. In the postseason, Freeman showed the heart of a champion. With his bat heating up at the right time, he delivered clutch hits and kept the Dodgers in games when it seemed like the momentum was shifting. Despite dealing with ongoing discomfort from his ankle injury, Freeman's determination never wavered. He kept pushing forward, not only to lead by example on the field but to inspire his teammates to keep fighting.

Freeman's role as both a player and a leader was never more evident than in the Dodgers' run to the World Series. His ability to play through pain, paired with his clutch performances, earned him the admiration of his teammates and the respect of the entire baseball community.

Chapter 2: A Night to Remember – Game 1 of the 2024 World Series

Pre-Game Buzz and the Atmosphere at Dodger Stadium

The atmosphere at Dodger Stadium on the night of Game 1 of the 2024 World Series was nothing short of electric. Fans packed the stands, their excitement palpable as they eagerly awaited the first pitch. The iconic stadium, a historic landmark in the baseball world, had a distinct buzz that could be felt from the parking lots to the concourses. There was a sense of anticipation in the air that only the Fall Classic can produce.

The energy surrounding the game wasn't just from the fans. Both teams were well aware of the magnitude of this matchup. The Dodgers, eager to bring another championship home to Los Angeles, were ready to capitalize on their home-field advantage. The Yankees, however, were hungry for redemption and primed to disrupt the Dodgers' momentum with their blend of veteran poise and youthful energy.

Before the first pitch, a palpable sense of history hung over the stadium. Fans reflected on the great moments the Dodgers had already created in the postseason, but tonight was about what lay ahead. Players took their positions on the field, the fans roared their support, and the night sky above Dodger Stadium set the stage for what promised to be a legendary game.

The opening ceremonies, complete with the singing of the national anthem, only added to the electricity. The color and grandeur of the pre-game festivities heightened the sense of occasion, marking the start of a World Series that promised to go down in the history books.

The Pitchers' Duel: Gerrit Cole vs. Jack Flaherty

Game 1's excitement hinged not only on the atmosphere in the stands but on the elite pitchers who would be taking the mound. For the Yankees, all eyes were on Gerrit Cole, a pitcher known for his power and precision. Cole had been the backbone of the Yankees' rotation throughout the season, consistently delivering standout performances when his team needed him most. His ability to control the game with his fastball and sharp breaking pitches made him a nightmare for opposing hitters. Coming into this game, Cole knew the weight on his shoulders—this wasn't just any regular-season game, it was the World Series.

For the Dodgers, Jack Flaherty was entrusted with the responsibility of leading the charge on the mound. Flaherty, a former All-Star with a fierce competitive streak, had proven himself capable of handling big moments. His ability to mix pitches and keep batters off balance would be crucial in a game where every at-bat could shift the momentum. Flaherty's fastball, combined with his slider and curveball, made him a formidable opponent. However, the World Series spotlight added a different level of pressure, and it would be his ability to remain composed that could determine the game's outcome.

As the game progressed, it was evident that this would be a classic pitchers' duel. Cole brought his best stuff, repeatedly getting out of jams with his characteristic poise and power. Flaherty, however, wasn't intimidated. He countered with his own electric stuff, keeping the Yankees' bats in check. Both pitchers demonstrated why they were in the game's brightest spotlight, giving their teams everything they had on the mound.

The duel between Cole and Flaherty wasn't just a battle of pitching, but a chess match of adjustments.

Every pitch was calculated; every decision was pivotal. Both pitchers fought tooth and nail, not just for the win but for the glory of leading their teams to an early advantage in the series.

Key Plays That Set the Stage for Extra Innings

As the game progressed, it became clear that Game 1 would not be settled easily. The defenses were sharp, and the pitching was near-perfect. However, a few key moments in the game helped set the stage for extra innings, making this an unforgettable battle.

The first key moment came in the top of the 7th inning when Flaherty found himself in a tight spot. With two Yankees on base and one out, he had to dig deep to keep the game scoreless. After a tense at-bat, Flaherty executed a flawless strikeout and then induced a grounder to end the threat. The crowd erupted as he walked off the mound, pumping his fist in triumph. The Dodgers had survived the inning unscathed, but the pressure remained high.

Not to be outdone, Cole responded in the bottom of the 8th inning with a critical strikeout of Mookie Betts, who had been a menace at the plate throughout the postseason. Cole's precision was on full display, as he hit his spots, painting the corners of the strike zone. This moment was pivotal, as the Dodgers were desperately trying to break the tie before the game went into extras. Despite Betts' prowess at the plate, Cole stood firm, securing the strikeout and keeping the game tied.

The final defining play that set the stage for extra innings came in the top of the 9th, when the Yankees loaded the bases with no outs. It was a moment of immense pressure, but Flaherty rose to the challenge, striking out two Yankees in quick succession. A pop-out to the shortstop soon followed, and the Dodgers escaped the jam. The defense had been impeccable, and both pitchers had shown their mettle under pressure, setting up the intense finale of this game.

As the game moved into extra innings, the tension was palpable. Both teams had fought tooth and nail, and it was clear that Game 1 was far from over. The stage had been set for a historic finish, and everyone in Dodger Stadium knew that the next few innings could be a defining moment in the 2024 World Series.

Chapter 3: The Build-Up to the Grand Slam

Late-Game Drama: Defensive Brilliance and Costly Mistakes

As the game wore on, the tension continued to rise, each inning more crucial than the last. The players on both teams seemed to understand the weight of every play, knowing that one small mistake could determine the outcome of the game. With the score still tied in the later innings, every pitch became a battle, and every defensive play was scrutinized for its impact on the game.

One of the key moments that set the stage for the drama to unfold came in the top of the 10th inning. With the Yankees threatening to break the tie, the Dodgers' defense stepped up in a big way. The infield was sharp, and the outfielders positioned themselves perfectly to stop any would-be rallies. A particularly critical play came from shortstop, who made a stunning, diving stop to prevent a potential base hit that could have loaded the bases. The crowd held its breath as the Dodgers executed a textbook double play to end the inning, preserving the tie and sending the game to the bottom of the 10th.

However, not all of the drama was positive. As the game progressed, both teams had moments of misfortune—critical mistakes that put added pressure on their defenses. A missed throw in the 9th inning allowed a Yankees runner to take an extra base, an error that could have proven costly. Meanwhile, a crucial passed ball in the 10th inning had the potential to allow a runner to score. But in both cases, the errors were either mitigated by stellar pitching or recovered by solid defensive plays, leaving fans on the edge of their seats.

What was clear, however, was that these small mistakes were quickly overshadowed by moments of brilliance. The Dodgers and Yankees both knew that one mistake could lead to disaster, but they also knew how to bounce back and keep the game alive. This balance of tension and relief built up the anticipation for what would be the final, dramatic play that would determine the outcome of the game.

Strategic Calls: Bringing in Nestor Cortes

In such a high-stakes game, every decision made by the coaches and managers was magnified. One of the most pivotal moments of Game 1 came when Yankees manager Aaron Boone made the decision to call upon Nestor Cortes in the later innings. Known for his unique pitching style and unpredictable delivery, Cortes had been a key asset to the Yankees all season long. However, bringing him in during the pressure of extra innings was a calculated gamble that could either make or break the game for New York.

Cortes had been excellent in relief during the regular season, and Boone trusted him to handle the situation. His pitching style, with its deceptive windup and varied pitches, was designed to keep hitters off balance. But the pressure of facing some of the best hitters in the league, with the game hanging in the balance, would put Cortes to the test. The decision to bring him in was bold, especially with the Yankees' bullpen already having worked hard in earlier innings, but Boone's confidence in his reliever was clear. Cortes would be tasked with getting out of a jam and preventing the Dodgers from scoring in the bottom of the 10th.

As Cortes took the mound, his focus was evident. He struck out the first batter he faced with ease, showcasing his craftiness. But the tension wasn't over. With runners on base and a loud Dodger crowd behind them, Cortes needed to keep his cool and deliver. The Yankees needed him to get through the inning without allowing any damage—and the tension built with each pitch. Every ball, every strike had the crowd roaring with anticipation. The strategy was clear: Cortes had to be nearly flawless to hold off the Dodgers' explosive offense.

But despite his best efforts, the Dodgers' offense remained undeterred. Cortes would face his toughest challenge yet when Freddie Freeman came to the plate.

Freddie Freeman's Resolve: Playing Through Pain

One of the most compelling storylines in this Game 1 was the resilience of Freddie Freeman. The Dodgers' star first baseman had been battling through an ankle injury throughout the postseason, and his performance in Game 1 was nothing short of heroic. It was clear that Freeman wasn't at 100 percent—he was visibly limping at times, and there were moments when it seemed the pain might catch up to him. Yet, despite the discomfort, Freeman remained determined, focusing on the bigger picture: leading his team to victory.

Freeman's resolve was tested in the bottom of the 10th inning when he stepped up to the plate with two outs and the game on the line. His ankle, which had been giving him trouble for weeks, appeared to be a significant hindrance. However, his veteran composure and experience in clutch moments allowed him to focus entirely on the task ahead, blocking out the pain in order to help his team. His at-bat would prove to be one of the most pivotal moments in World Series history.

Despite being hobbled, Freeman's bat remained lethal. He had a patient approach at the plate, waiting for the right pitch. Cortes, for all his deception, could not outlast Freeman's resolve. With two runners on base and the game on the line, Freeman's disciplined approach paid off. He swung at a hanging slider, sending it over the fence for a walk-off grand slam—one of the most dramatic and memorable moments in baseball postseason history. The crowd erupted in ecstasy as Freeman rounded the bases, his injury momentarily forgotten in the wake of his heroics.

The moment was pure baseball magic. Freeman's grand slam wasn't just a physical accomplishment—it was a testament to his determination, mental toughness, and leadership. Despite battling injury, Freeman's ability to rise to the occasion and deliver in the most clutch of moments solidified his place as a baseball legend.

Chapter 4: The Walk-Off Grand Slam

Analyzing the At-Bat: Freeman vs. Cortes

The bottom of the 10th inning in Game 1 of the 2024 World Series was an unforgettable moment in baseball history. The stage was set for Freddie Freeman, the Los Angeles Dodgers' star first baseman, to face off against New York Yankees' pitcher Nestor Cortes. With two runners on base and the game tied, the stakes couldn't have been higher. Freeman, playing through the pain of a lingering ankle injury, stood tall in the batter's box, fully aware that the outcome of this at-bat would determine the course of the game—and possibly the series.

Cortes, known for his unorthodox pitching style, took to the mound with a clear mission: to shut down Freeman and prevent the Dodgers from walking off with the game. His deceptive delivery and pitch variety were his strengths, but against a seasoned hitter like Freeman, who had seen it all, even Cortes' best pitches could be in danger of being put in play. Freeman, though not at full strength, wasn't going to be easily fooled. His experience and patience at the plate were on full display as he carefully evaluated each pitch thrown his way.

The at-bat started with a series of well-placed pitches from Cortes, who kept Freeman off balance. However, Freeman was patient, showing excellent discipline, and didn't rush to swing at anything that wasn't in his zone. He had been in enough big moments to know that a walk would put the game-winning run on base, but it was clear that Freeman wanted more—he wanted to be the hero. As the count advanced, Freeman was presented with a key pitch: a slider that hung just a bit too high in the strike zone. With one swift motion, Freeman made contact, and the ball shot off his bat toward the outfield.

It was a moment that could be described as a perfect storm of timing, technique, and sheer determination. Despite the lingering injury, Freeman's swing was as fluid and powerful as ever, and he had found the sweet spot of the bat just when his team needed him the most. The crack of the bat echoed through Dodger Stadium, and the ball sailed high, heading toward the outfield fence. Everyone watching knew that the game, and possibly the series, had just changed forever.

The Swing That Shocked the World: Crowd and Stadium Reaction

As the ball soared through the air, Dodger Stadium fell into an eerie silence for a split second, as all eyes were fixed on the flight of the ball. Would it clear the fence? Would Freeman's dream moment turn into a nightmare for the Yankees? But the answer came quickly. As the ball crossed the outfield wall and the crowd erupted into an explosion of noise, it became clear that Freeman had just made history.

The eruption from the Dodger fans was deafening. It was a feeling of pure ecstasy, a mix of disbelief and joy, as the realization sank in that Freeman had just hit the first-ever walk-off grand slam in World Series history. The stadium became a sea of blue as fans screamed, cheered, and waved their hands in celebration. Freeman, after briefly pausing to make sure the ball had indeed cleared the fence, took off running around the bases, his injury momentarily forgotten as the adrenaline took over.

As Freeman rounded third base, he was met by his teammates, who were equally stunned by the magnitude of the moment. The entire Dodgers dugout emptied in celebration, with every player rushing out to congratulate Freeman. It was a surreal moment for everyone watching, a historic milestone in a game that had already been filled with drama. Even the most experienced baseball fans in the stands could not fully grasp the significance of what they had just witnessed—history had been made.

The Yankees, on the other hand, stood in shock, their hopes of securing a victory dashed by Freeman's clutch swing. Cortes, who had pitched valiantly, stood on the mound with a look of disbelief. He had thrown his best pitches, but in the end, it wasn't enough to stop Freeman from etching his name into the history books.

Making History: The First Walk-Off Slam in World Series History

Freddie Freeman's grand slam wasn't just another home run—it was a moment that would be forever etched in the annals of baseball. This was the first walk-off grand slam in World Series history, an achievement so rare and so significant that it immediately became a part of the sport's rich lore. To make history in such a dramatic fashion is a rare feat, and for Freeman, it was a culmination of years of hard work, perseverance, and unrelenting passion for the game.

The significance of Freeman's grand slam goes beyond the physical act of hitting a baseball out of the park. It was a moment that symbolized everything that makes baseball great: the tension, the strategy, the physical prowess, and the mental fortitude. In a high-pressure situation, Freeman stood tall, playing through injury, and delivered a swing that would forever define his legacy.

The historic nature of the walk-off grand slam was not lost on anyone who had witnessed it. Baseball is a sport that thrives on moments of tension and brilliance, and Freeman's grand slam encapsulated all of that. It was a testament to his strength as both a player and a leader—a player who had fought through adversity all season long to be in that moment. For the Dodgers, it was a moment of redemption and hope, one that set the tone for the rest of the series. For the Yankees, it was a harsh reminder that in a game of inches, one swing could change everything.

The walk-off grand slam will be remembered for generations. It was a milestone not only for Freeman but for baseball as a whole. His name will forever be associated with one of the most iconic moments in World Series history, a moment that captured the very essence of what it means to rise to the occasion and deliver when the stakes are highest.

Chapter 5: The Aftermath and Reactions

Post-Game Insights: Freeman, Teammates, and Dave Roberts Speak Out

In the immediate aftermath of Freddie Freeman's historic walk-off grand slam, the Dodgers' locker room was filled with a mixture of disbelief, jubilation, and gratitude. Freeman, who had just delivered one of the most memorable moments in baseball history, was quick to give credit to his teammates and the Dodgers' organization. Despite his individual glory, Freeman stressed the collective effort that had propelled the team to such an emotional victory. "This moment is bigger than just me," he remarked in his post-game interview. "It's about this team, our resilience, and our ability to never give up, no matter the circumstances."

His teammates echoed his sentiment. Veteran players like Mookie Betts and Clayton Kershaw, who had been part of numerous playoff runs with the Dodgers, were equally impressed by Freeman's ability to rise to the occasion, especially considering his ongoing injury struggles. Betts, always the optimist, couldn't help but smile as he spoke about the at-bat. "That's why Freddie is here," he said. "He's a big-time player, and he stepped up when we needed him most." The camaraderie in the locker room was palpable, with players congratulating each other and recognizing that Game 1 was a statement win for the entire team.

Dodgers manager Dave Roberts also took a moment to reflect on the historic nature of the game. He had managed through countless high-pressure moments, but the energy in the stadium after Freeman's grand slam was unlike anything he had experienced. "As a manager, moments like this are why you do what you do," Roberts said. "Freddie's performance tonight was something special, and it's a testament to his character, his leadership, and his work ethic. We're all just lucky to be along for the ride." Roberts' words underscored the magnitude of the moment—not just for Freeman, but for the team as a whole.

Yankees' Reflection: Aaron Boone's Decisions Under Scrutiny

While the Dodgers were celebrating, the Yankees were left to contemplate what could have been. The loss stung, especially after their valiant efforts throughout the game. For Yankees manager Aaron Boone, the walk-off grand slam marked a tough moment of reflection. As much as the Yankees had fought back and put themselves in a position to win, the decision to bring in Nestor Cortes in such a high-stakes situation was quickly called into question.

Boone, who had been criticized in the past for some of his managerial decisions, was once again under the microscope. The choice to stick with Cortes, despite the pitcher's long outing earlier in the game, seemed questionable in hindsight. While Cortes had delivered solid innings up until that point, the Dodgers' lineup, particularly Freeman, had been growing more aggressive. Many felt that Boone might have been better served by bringing in a fresh arm, one capable of handling the pressure that came with extra innings and a full Dodger Stadium crowd. The decision to let Cortes face Freeman, who had been battling injuries but was still a force at the plate, raised eyebrows among fans and analysts alike.

"I trust Nestor, but that's one of those decisions where you wonder if the outcome would have been different if we had gone with someone else," Boone said in his post-game comments. The second-guessing didn't stop there, as critics in the media and on social platforms debated the merits of

Boone's decision and whether it contributed to the Yankees' downfall in Game 1. For Boone, it was a tough loss, but he took responsibility for the outcome, acknowledging that as the manager, the ultimate blame fell on his shoulders.

The Moment That Broke the Internet: Media and Fan Reactions

Freddie Freeman's walk-off grand slam wasn't just a moment for the players on the field—it was a moment that captivated the world. The internet exploded with reactions from fans, analysts, and sports outlets, all sharing their awe and excitement about the historic play. Social media platforms like Twitter, Instagram, and Facebook were flooded with posts, memes, and videos of the grand slam, each post gaining traction as the story spread far beyond Dodger fans and Yankees supporters.

For sports fans, this wasn't just about the Dodgers' victory—it was about the game itself. Freeman's swing, his grit, and the dramatic circumstances surrounding the game made it an instant classic. Clips of the at-bat were replayed endlessly, from all angles, with fans and commentators analyzing every detail. The hashtag #FreddieFreeman quickly trended on Twitter, with people from all walks of life joining in the celebration. It wasn't just about the Dodgers; it was about a moment that transcended the game of baseball and united fans everywhere in a shared appreciation for the beauty of sports.

Media outlets also seized on the grand slam's significance. The game became a top story, with sports analysts and commentators taking to television and podcasts to discuss the implications of Freeman's historic hit. Even the casual sports fan who might not follow the World Series closely found themselves captivated by the excitement surrounding the moment. The walk-off grand slam quickly became a viral sensation, with major sports websites and news outlets reporting on the play and breaking down the emotions of the players involved.

On the other side, Yankees fans were also vocal in their reactions, voicing both their frustration with the loss and their disbelief over the game's outcome. Social media posts from Yankees supporters reflected disappointment but also admiration for Freeman's clutch performance. For many, it was a bitter pill to swallow, but even they couldn't deny the greatness of what they had witnessed.

By the end of the night, the world had witnessed one of the most dramatic and historical moments in recent World Series history, and the internet had responded in kind, elevating the grand slam to legendary status. The moment broke the internet not just because of the play, but because it was a moment that reminded us all why we love sports:

the unpredictability, the passion, and the larger-than-life heroes who emerge when the pressure is at its highest.

Chapter 6: Echoes of the Past

Reliving Kirk Gibson's Iconic 1988 Walk-Off Home Run

For fans of the Los Angeles Dodgers, the 1988 World Series remains one of the most unforgettable moments in baseball history. Kirk Gibson's dramatic, limping walk-off home run in Game 1 of that series against the Oakland Athletics is etched in the memories of those who witnessed it, standing as one of the defining moments in World Series lore. The game itself had already been a hard-fought battle, with the Dodgers trailing 4-3 in the bottom of the ninth inning, but when Gibson came to the plate, few expected what was about to unfold.

The powerful swing that sent the ball soaring into the night, while Gibson hobbled around the bases due to a knee injury, was a symbol of grit and determination. His iconic fist pump as he rounded third base was not just a celebration of the home run but also of an athlete's resolve to overcome obstacles and seize a moment. That swing became an indelible image, forever linking Gibson to the Dodgers' World Series victories and baseball fans everywhere.

As the years have passed, the story of Gibson's walk-off has only grown in significance. It's more than just a home run—it's a moment that captures the very essence of what makes baseball so special. The drama, the emotion, and the history of it all combine to make it one of the most celebrated moments in sports. For those watching Freddie Freeman's grand slam in 2024, the echoes of Gibson's home run must have been present in their minds. Both moments showcased the power of clutch performances and the unpredictable nature of the game—two walks off the grand stage that captivated audiences and created lasting memories.

Revisiting the Dodgers-Yankees Rivalry in World Series History

The 2024 World Series is not just another chapter in baseball's history; it's a rekindling of one of the most storied rivalries in sports: the Los Angeles Dodgers versus the New York Yankees. These two teams have met in the World Series before, with their first clash dating back to 1941, when the Yankees defeated the Dodgers in five games. The rivalry has since evolved, with the teams facing off in 1947, 1952, 1953, and later in 1977 and 1978. Each series added layers to the rivalry, fueling the animosity between two of baseball's most iconic franchises.

The Yankees have long been known for their dominance in the World Series, with their 27 championships standing as a testament to their success. On the other hand, the Dodgers have built a legacy of their own, particularly with their recent successes and iconic players. The blend of historical significance and modern-day excellence makes any encounter between these teams an instant classic, but the 2024 series holds a special place. The Dodgers' pursuit of another title and the Yankees' quest for redemption from past heartbreaks give this series an added level of tension and excitement.

The World Series encounters between these teams have always been more than just a battle for a championship; they represent the heart and soul of baseball's competitive spirit. The Dodgers and Yankees have met at pivotal points in the sport's history, often facing each other with rosters that featured some of the best players ever to play the game. Whether it was Jackie Robinson in the early years, Sandy Koufax in the 1960s, or Reggie Jackson's unforgettable performances in the 1970s, the history of the Dodgers-Yankees rivalry is marked by unforgettable performances and a fierce desire to win.

As the 2024 World Series unfolds, the rivalry takes on new layers. It's not just about adding another trophy to the shelf for either team; it's about cementing a legacy, one that resonates across generations of fans who have watched these two teams go head-to-head. The history between the Dodgers and Yankees brings with it a sense of anticipation, as the echoes of past matchups remind fans that every pitch, every swing, and every play carries the weight of that rich legacy.

Honoring Fernando Valenzuela: A Tribute to a Dodgers Legend

Amid the excitement of the 2024 World Series, it's impossible not to reflect on the legacy of one of the most beloved figures in Dodgers history: Fernando Valenzuela. Known for his dazzling performances on the mound and his unique delivery, Valenzuela captivated fans during the 1980s and became a symbol of hope and pride, particularly within the Mexican-American community. His rise to prominence as a young pitcher was nothing short of remarkable, and his impact on the Dodgers was profound.

Valenzuela's "Fernandomania" swept across Los Angeles in 1981, as he led the Dodgers to a World Series title and captured the hearts of fans with his mastery on the mound. His signature screwball baffled hitters and made him one of the most feared pitchers of his era. But beyond his statistical accomplishments, Valenzuela's influence extended far beyond the diamond. He became a cultural icon, bridging gaps and uniting fans from all walks of life. In a city as diverse as Los Angeles, Valenzuela's success was a beacon of hope for many, showing that dreams could come true no matter your background.

As the Dodgers play in the 2024 World Series, it's important to recognize the trail that figures like

Valenzuela blazed. He helped establish the team's
enduring legacy and contributed to the
development of Latino players in Major League
Baseball. The Dodgers organization has never
forgotten Valenzuela's contributions, frequently
honoring him during special events and
commemorations. Even decades after his time with
the team, Valenzuela remains a beloved figure in
Dodgers history, with his number 34 immortalized
in the minds of fans.

In 2024, as the Dodgers pursue another World
Series championship, the memories of Valenzuela's
accomplishments serve as a reminder of the team's
storied past and the players who helped shape it.
It's not just about the victories on the field; it's
about the enduring influence of players like
Fernando Valenzuela, who brought a sense of pride
and passion to the game and left a lasting mark on
the sport.

Chapter 7: A Series to Remember

Game 1's Influence on the Rest of the 2024 World Series

The dramatic Game 1 of the 2024 World Series between the Los Angeles Dodgers and the New York Yankees set the stage for what would become an unforgettable series. A game full of emotion, unforgettable plays, and pivotal moments, Game 1 was more than just a single contest—it was a tone-setter. The energy in the stadium, fueled by Freddie Freeman's walk-off grand slam, reverberated throughout the entire series, and it quickly became clear that the outcome of Game 1 would have a lasting impact on how both teams would approach the following games.

For the Dodgers, the momentum from the win provided an emotional boost, making them feel invincible going forward. The unforgettable grand slam gave the team confidence and the belief that no situation was too daunting. For the Yankees, however, it was a harsh reminder of how quickly things could turn. While the Yankees had strong players and a wealth of experience, the crushing loss in Game 1 forced them to regroup and adjust. Game 1 wasn't just about the outcome—it was about the mental game that would unfold over the course of the series.

The psychological toll of such a dramatic loss can't be overstated. The Yankees had to quickly put that disappointment behind them and return to the game with a renewed sense of purpose. For the Dodgers, the win was a rallying cry—a signal that they had what it took to overcome any challenge. As the series progressed, the shadow of Game 1 continued to loom large, influencing everything from strategy to player performances, keeping fans on the edge of their seats.

Standout Performances in the Following Games

After the emotional intensity of Game 1, the following games continued to be a battle of wills, filled with unforgettable moments and standout performances that shaped the course of the 2024 World Series.

For the Dodgers, several players rose to the occasion, building on the momentum gained in Game 1. Freddie Freeman, already a hero from his walk-off grand slam, remained a key figure throughout the series. His leadership and consistency at the plate helped keep the Dodgers' offense firing on all cylinders. However, it wasn't just Freeman who contributed. Players like Mookie

Betts and Will Smith also played pivotal roles, providing timely hits and strong defense. The Dodgers' pitching staff also stepped up, delivering performances that kept the Yankees' potent lineup in check and ensured the Dodgers could stay competitive in every game.

On the other side, the Yankees were far from out of the fight. Despite their tough loss in Game 1, they had an arsenal of talent capable of turning the tide at any moment. Gerrit Cole, one of the most dominant pitchers in baseball, delivered some of his most stellar performances, making his presence known in the postseason once again. Aaron Judge, the Yankees' star hitter, continued to display his raw power and ability to change the game with a single swing. As the series wore on, it became clear that the Yankees weren't going down without a fight.

Standout performances came from unexpected places as well. Dodgers pitchers like Clayton

Kershaw and Julio Urías proved their mettle on the mound, showcasing their experience and ability to perform under pressure. Likewise, Yankees' players like Anthony Rizzo and Giancarlo Stanton had moments where they seemed poised to turn the series in New York's favor, providing the kind of power that could swing the momentum.

These performances—both expected and surprising—made every game feel unpredictable, with each play adding another layer to the drama that was unfolding before fans' eyes. By the time the World Series moved into the later games, both teams had proven that no lead was safe, and every inning mattered.

The Dodgers' Pursuit of Championship Glory

As the series advanced, the Dodgers' pursuit of their long-awaited championship title continued to shine through. The 2024 World Series was more than just another chance to add to the team's storied history; it was a reflection of years of growth, determination, and resilience. For a franchise that had been close so many times but had fallen short, the drive to secure another title was palpable in every pitch and every at-bat.

The Dodgers' pursuit was led by veteran leadership and key players like Freeman, Betts, and Kershaw, but it was the collective effort of the entire roster that proved to be their most potent weapon. Every player understood the importance of the moment, and that sense of urgency pushed them to rise to the occasion. From gritty defensive plays to clutch hits in key moments, the Dodgers displayed the kind of cohesion that championship teams are made of.

At the same time, the Dodgers faced the weight of their own history. Fans who had watched the team go through painful postseason losses in years past knew that this World Series was their opportunity to finally push through and seize the ultimate prize. The pressure of such expectations was never far from the players' minds, but it never seemed to overwhelm them. Instead, it became the driving force that fueled their performances. The 2024 World Series was shaping up to be a defining moment in the franchise's rich legacy, one that could potentially add another chapter to the tale of the Dodgers' greatness.

While the Yankees were certainly formidable opponents, the Dodgers' sense of purpose was clear. They weren't just playing for the trophy; they were playing for the history books. Every pitch, every swing, every defensive play had a deeper meaning in their pursuit of the one thing that had eluded them for years—a World Series title.

Chapter 8: Freddie Freeman's Legacy

Cementing His Status in Dodgers and Baseball History

Freddie Freeman's journey to becoming a Dodgers legend is one marked by consistent excellence, unwavering leadership, and an unrelenting drive to win. His arrival in Los Angeles in 2022, after spending over a decade with the Atlanta Braves, was met with high expectations. Yet, Freeman quickly became more than just a key acquisition for the Dodgers. He became the heart and soul of the team, a beacon of consistency and professionalism.

His performance in the 2024 World Series only solidified his place in Dodgers' history. The walk-off grand slam in Game 1 will forever be etched in the annals of baseball, not just for its dramatic timing but for its symbolism of Freeman's clutch gene. In a series where both teams fought tooth and nail, Freeman's game-winning hit was a reflection of his growth as a player—someone who embraces the big moment and thrives under pressure.

Freeman's ability to step up when it mattered most has given him a legacy that stretches far beyond the boundaries of a single World Series. His place among the Dodgers' greats like Jackie Robinson, Sandy Koufax, and Clayton Kershaw is no longer a matter of "if," but "when." His career numbers and the consistency he's displayed over the years place him among the most respected hitters in the game. As one of the cornerstones of the Dodgers, Freeman's legacy is now fully cemented, and his impact on the franchise and baseball as a whole will be felt for generations to come.

Overcoming Obstacles: A Career Defined by Resilience

Freddie Freeman's path to baseball stardom has never been a smooth ride. From the very beginning of his career, he faced challenges that would have derailed many players. Drafted by the Atlanta Braves as a young hopeful, Freeman had to work through the ups and downs of the minor leagues before eventually establishing himself as one of the premier first basemen in Major League Baseball.

Throughout his career, Freeman's resilience has been a defining trait. He's been tested on the field, facing tough pitching, long seasons, and the mental strain that comes with being a star. But perhaps the most significant challenge came off the field in 2021 when Freeman dealt with the loss of his mother, a pivotal moment in his life. Yet, rather than crumbling under the weight of grief, Freeman found a way to honor his mother's memory by channeling his emotions into his performance on the field. It was a testament to his character and ability to overcome life's most difficult obstacles.

In addition to personal adversity, Freeman has faced the physical demands of playing at the highest level. Injuries, especially early in his career, threatened to limit his potential, but Freeman's work ethic and perseverance allowed him to bounce back each time stronger. It's these moments of adversity that have shaped his career and made his triumphs even sweeter. Through it all, Freeman has been a model of resilience, showing that greatness is often built through overcoming challenges rather than avoiding them.

The Lasting Impact of His Historic Grand Slam

While Freddie Freeman's legacy extends far beyond a single moment, his walk-off grand slam in Game 1 of the 2024 World Series will forever be remembered as one of the most iconic plays in baseball history. The timing, the stakes, and the opponent all made this moment unforgettable. But it was Freeman's leadership and calm under pressure that truly defined the play.

The grand slam wasn't just a game-winner; it was a symbol of Freeman's larger impact on the game. His ability to perform when the lights are brightest has now become part of his identity as a player. As fans erupted in celebration, Freeman's teammates rushed the field, and the collective roar of Dodger Stadium reverberated through the night air. It wasn't just a walk-off—it was a moment that encapsulated everything Freeman had worked for throughout his career: a chance to make history when his team needed him most.

This grand slam, in many ways, is the culmination of Freeman's career. It was a moment that sealed his place in baseball folklore, ensuring that he would always be remembered as a player who delivered in the most dramatic of circumstances. As future generations of fans watch replays of that historic play, they'll not only witness a grand slam but will also learn about the character of a player who embodied the spirit of baseball. Freeman's grand slam will remain a testament to the kind of player he is—one who rises above the moment, delivers when called upon, and leaves a lasting legacy in the sport.

Conclusion

Reflections on an Unforgettable Moment in Baseball

The 2024 World Series will forever be remembered for its drama, intensity, and one unforgettable moment that transcended the game itself. Freddie Freeman's walk-off grand slam in Game 1 has carved its place in baseball history, a moment that captured the hearts of fans around the world. It wasn't just the thrill of a walk-off; it was the magnitude of the situation—a high-stakes postseason game with everything on the line. The crack of the bat, the rise of the crowd, and the sheer joy of witnessing a piece of baseball history unfold before their eyes made it a night to remember for Dodgers fans and sports fans alike.

This grand slam was more than just a highlight in a single game; it represented the epitome of baseball's ability to deliver moments of pure emotion. It was a showcase of the passion that drives the sport, the fierce competitiveness of the players, and the bond between a team and its fans. The moment symbolized the essence of what makes baseball unique—a game where one play can change everything, where the outcome of a single swing can decide a legacy. Freeman's hit wasn't merely a play; it was a celebration of the very spirit of the game.

The Legacy of Freeman's Grand Slam in World Series Lore

As the years pass, Freeman's grand slam will be remembered alongside some of the greatest plays in World Series history. It wasn't just a walk-off hit; it was the first-ever walk-off grand slam in World Series history, cementing its place in the sport's storied tradition. When future generations of fans reminisce about the 2024 World Series, that moment will be highlighted as one of the key turning points, a play that exemplified the Dodgers' resilience and their pursuit of greatness.

Freddie Freeman's name will be forever linked to this moment, a lasting symbol of his clutch gene and his ability to deliver in the most critical of situations. As the first baseman who stepped up when the Dodgers needed him most, his grand slam will be seen as a testament to his skill, composure, and leadership. The legacy of this play will not fade with time; instead, it will become a benchmark for future stars who strive to leave their own mark on the game. In years to come, Freeman's grand slam will be replayed during postseason highlight reels, continuing to inspire players, fans, and baseball enthusiasts.

Looking Ahead: The Dodgers, Freddie Freeman, and the Rivalry's Future

While the 2024 World Series was a defining chapter for both the Dodgers and Freddie Freeman, the future holds even more promise. The Dodgers, with their rich history and relentless pursuit of championships, are poised to remain a powerhouse in the MLB for years to come. With Freeman at the heart of their lineup, the team's championship aspirations are stronger than ever. Freeman's leadership and clutch performances are an invaluable asset, and his continued excellence will be crucial as the team builds on its success in the coming seasons.

The rivalry between the Dodgers and the Yankees, two of the most iconic franchises in the sport, also shows no signs of slowing down. With both teams consistently at the top of their respective divisions, fans can expect more thrilling matchups in the years to come. The drama between these two teams is far from over, and moments like Freeman's grand slam will only add fuel to the fire, deepening the history and intensity of this historic rivalry.

As the Dodgers and Freeman continue their pursuit of more championships, one thing is certain: the 2024 World Series will remain a defining moment, both for the team and for the man who made it unforgettable. For Freeman, the legacy of his grand slam is just one chapter in what is shaping up to be a legendary career. And for Dodgers fans, the excitement surrounding the team's future is only just beginning.

Made in United States
Troutdale, OR
12/21/2024

27055915R00040